# opening

### the

## STABLE
## DOOR

soulation PRESS

"Yes," said Queen Lucy. "In our world too, a stable once had something inside it that was bigger than our whole world."

*The Last Battle*, C.S. Lewis

# TABLE
## *of*
# CONTENTS

## Week 1 :: HOPE

*He has raised up a horn of salvation for us in the house
of his servant David.*

### Sunday

A Speechless Priest

### Wednesday

Our Epic Hero

### Friday

Sounds of Certainty

## Week 2 :: PEACE

*Many are asking, "Who can show us any good?"
Let the light of your face shine upon us, O LORD.*

### Sunday

Close Encounters

### Wednesday

Gift of Vulnerability

### Friday

Winter without Christmas

## Week 3 :: JOY

*Do not be afraid. I bring you good news of great joy*
*that will be for all the people.*

---

### Sunday
The Traveler's Feet

### Wednesday
Welcome to Tinseltown

### Friday
Star of Wonder

## Week 4 :: LOVE

*For God so loved the world that he sent his only begotten son.*

---

### Sunday
Custom-Made Care

### Wednesday
No Minutes to Spare

### Friday
Love Needs Knowledge

## Christmas Eve :: MESSIAH

---

### Christmas Eve
Light in Darkness

# INTRODUCTION

We shop and plan, eat and dress up, and then the Christmas holiday is over. The day after Christmas finds us sitting on couches in a sort of coma, waiting for the New Year, dreading the resumption of 9-to-5 jobs.

We at Soulation want to change the way we all do Christmas preparation. Open these pages to find Soulation meditations on Hope, Peace, Joy, and Love, written without schmaltz or worn-out words, to guide you through the four weeks of advent. Be prepared to watch your heart open and have your mind strengthened as you read winsome apologetics and accessible spiritual formation centered on Jesus' birth.

Our intention is not to overwhelm you, but to encourage you to pause three times each week, and pay attention to the things that often get crowded out in the holiday hoopla. Christmas tells us that God doesn't regret making us. Jesus' arrival means humans are pretty loveable stuff, fine enough for the Logos to incarnate and make new.

This season we get to notice how to become more appropriately human, like our Savior who took on flesh without reservation, arriving around cows and sheep, in a small room with unwed parents.

*Merry Christmas!*

**Dale and Jonalyn Fincher**

hope

## A Speechless Priest
*By Dale Fincher*

Abraham doubted. Gideon doubted. Thomas doubted. Even Mary, the mother of Jesus, had her questions for the angel. So what made Zechariah different? Why were the vocal cords of this faithful priest muted, while many other doubters in scripture suffer far less consequence?

Anytime I read Luke's opening chapter, I chase this tension around, wondering why Zechariah, why the temporary curse? I suspect it was the lack of belief with so much evidence. Some commentators say that in ancient Israel the opportunity to perform priestly duty in the Holy Place would come only once in a priest's career. This was Zechariah's highest moment. Then suddenly Gabriel, the angel who always brings dramatically good news, appears and tells Zechariah that he will have a son. Zechariah has two pieces of information to put against this proclamation: he is old and his wife has been barren since her youth. But apparently God is unimpressed with little bits of impossibilities. He wants eyes on the big picture, to remember that this is the God whose biography is littered with evidence of faithfulness.

Surrounding Zechariah was the second most holy place on the planet. (The Holy of Holies, which lay beyond the curtain, was first). He could see the monuments reminding him of God's faithfulness to his people: bread, incense, and candlesticks. There was the veil separating him from God's presence. Even more, Gabriel stood looking at him eye to eye. The character of God, the testimony of God, and the work of God all overshadowed Zechariah's little dilemmas. Yet perhaps Zechariah had resigned to be childless. His disposition may have already been bitterly fixed.

God offers, as a consequence, the perfect sign to the people outside. Had his punishment been a limp in the leg, Zechariah could have faked it. If it were a steady growth of leprosy, Zechariah could have hid it under his cloak. The people waiting outside expected the ritual blessing, and God offered a sign to them using the most ironic thing in Israel: a speechless priest. They knew immediately that something had happened in the temple. God was on the move.

God was on the move.

To add one more ironic note, the silent Zechariah begets the loudest voice in the spiritually-silent wilderness of Israel, John the Baptist. The prophet Isaiah proclaimed that one would make the pathway of the Messiah straight. Who would suspect it to be Jesus' own cousin?

When we see mangers as cribs and angels proclaiming to shepherds, we must remember that a larger story was in motion. God's orchestration of events went beyond the holy family making a pilgrimage on a donkey. A speechless high priest today, a condemning high priest tomorrow. A manger today, a cross tomorrow. And from all of these events, God brings Jesus into the Holy Family so that all families could be made holy who would hear the voice of God.

# Our Epic Hero
*By Dale Fincher*

Scholars tell us that Mark was the first of the four Gospels to be written. Apart from the oral testimony spreading throughout the land in those early decades of the church, and apart from the theology of Jesus mentioned in Paul's Epistles, Mark's Gospel was the first written story of Jesus on the ancient bookshelf.

The first scene of Jesus is found in verse nine of the first chapter: "In those days Jesus came…"

The hero steps into view. The cameras focus. Who is this guy? We expect something big.

Though I've read that passage many times, I enjoy re-reading it like I enjoy my favorite books. I know what's coming. I know what is said. I know the conclusion. I love to return to the beginning, to see our hero again for the first time. Each entrance is bigger and more thrilling to me because I know better who he is.

> I love to return to the beginning, to see our hero again for the first time.

For example, re-entering Narnia through the wardrobe with the Pevensie children remains a thrill. They discover the whole land has been enchanted by the White Witch. She has cast a spell so that it is always winter and never Christmas. Suddenly, thick in the woods, they encounter a talking beaver. He makes a statement that still burns in my imagination. "Aslan's on the move," he says. "And some say he's already landed." My heart races. The children do not know who Aslan is yet, but they do know it is good news. How good? The re-reader knows!

Again, in the same series, Lucy finds herself upon a voyage to the unknown Eastern Seas of Narnia. They are caught in a black mist upon the ocean and cannot find their way out. To add to the threat, they discover this is the island where the darkest of dreams come true. The crew scatters throughout the boat, rowing in circles, frantically trying to avoid any thought of the bad dreams they have had. But their dreams close in upon them. The darkness grows thicker. Lucy climbs to the top lookout and shouts, "Aslan, if ever you loved us, send us help now!" A light shines ahead, a flying thing approaches. Suddenly, with the whirring of wings, it comes clear: an Albatross. It guides them toward the bright world. But as it circles the mast, it speaks to Lucy and breathes on her. And she knows that it is Aslan himself.

These moments bring goose bumps.

When I begin the book of Mark, I find this same kind of drama. A great winter has been laid upon the earth. Darkness has closed in. The promises of God are made and the prayers of the ancients are heard. All is dark. The menorah is burning. "In those days Jesus came."

Pause and re-read. Pause and re-read. Frame the moment in your imagination. The great winter is about to thaw. Light has come to shine in the darkness. Our epic hero has landed.

Frame the moment in your imagination. The great winter is about to thaw.

# Sounds of certainty
*By Dale Fincher*

Hope is the thing that turns the heart upside-down in the middle of grief. Hope is the embers burning after the fire has gone out. Hope is the healthy spare tire in the trunk of the car with a flat.

Unlike the above examples, our modern use of the word "hope" no longer carries the biblical notion. It now carries a heart-cry of whimsical uncertainty or anxious waiting. As children we hope for a bicycle on Christmas morning. As adults we hope the colonoscopy brings back negative cancer results. In neither is there a promise.

When the Bible talks about hope, it often carries certainty with it. And like faith, it is necessary that the one making the promises has the kind of character and ability that can deliver on those promises.

> When the bible talks about hope, it often carries certainty with it.

What about Israel's King David? Where was his hope? God spoke to him in an ancient land. "Your house and your kingdom will endure forever before me; your throne will be established forever." David grabs hope and replies, "Your servant has found courage" because of the bold promise of God. David knew God's character was one that did not lie.1

Then a thousand years later, the New Testament writers shatter the silence and exclaim that, among many other prophecies, David's hope was born in his hometown. The angel, unhindered by the sentimentality of many holiday cards, moves to proclaim the mystery of the incarnation to a young virgin girl. Borrowing the same wording that God spoke to David, the angel comes to a lone individual to speak forth the fulfilled promise that consummated David's hope, "The Lord God will give [Jesus] the throne of his father David, and he will reign over the house of Jacob forever; his kingdom will never end."2

But the hope God gives in his promises are not solely for kings in ancient days. Jesus Christ uttered the certainty to his followers: "And if I go and prepare a place for you, I will come back and take you to be with me that you also may be where I am."3

There are, no doubt, many ready skeptics who find pleasure in calling this "wishful thinking." And there's a certain gladness in hope that is similar to the excitement of wishful thinking. But isn't that just the point? Why does my heart long so deeply for eternal hope and confidence if it is never to be gained? Why do longings for future glory have to be merely wishful? The skeptic who says such things about hope is often the one who has been burned by bad promises told by bad people. Does a broken promise mean the heart's desire is broken too? The heart still reaches for the right promise from an eternally unchanging character.

The writer of Hebrews understood this when he wrote, "We...have a strong consolation, who have fled for refuge to lay hold upon the hope set before us: which hope we have as an anchor of the soul, both sure and steadfast." The hope in Jesus Christ.4

Go with Mary into the place where the angel announces Jesus. Hear the angel tell of kept promises to David and the world. Go with the disciples into the room where Jesus promises his return. Go with the readers of Hebrews into the refuge that is found in the anchor of hope. And anticipate with wonder that God indeed visited our planet as a carpenter near Galilee and will come again without any disguises. May hope turn our hearts upside-down this celebration season because God has granted wishes long before we uttered them.

May hope turn our hearts upside-down

[1] *2 Samuel 7:16 NIV*
[2] *Luke 1:32-33 NIV*
[3] *John 14:3 NIV*
[4] *Hebrews 6:18-19 KJV*

peace

## Close encounters
*By Jonalyn Fincher*

The real Jesus is not like most of our pictures of him.

I think of a video from my first Christmas service without extended family. It had this goofy bit where Jesus meets Santa Claus. It was funny, but what bothered me was that the Jesus character wore a stringy, long, brown wig. He spoke in a monotone voice and looked anything but relevant or genuine. I was surprised when the pastor didn't comment on how this wasn't really the Jesus who spun the stars into orbit, or came as a baby, or died on the cross.

The real Jesus is not like most of our pictures of him.

It made me want to share how real I think Jesus is. Perhaps you've struggled like I have to see Jesus, to want to get beyond the guy with the wig and find out if this Christ guy is really worth all the fuss. He is so spiritual, which often means ghostly, irrelevant, unhelpful, and boring. We need to push the refresh button on "spiritual." We need new pictures of God.

In A Christmas Carol, Charles Dickens gives us

refreshing pictures of how REAL the spiritual world is.

Scrooge is visited by three spirits, not transparent, white, or flimsy beings either. They are real and powerful, but immaterial (they are not made of matter). These ghosts are SPIRITual. The Spirit of Christmas Present is so authentic that I want you to see what he's like. Perhaps this Ghost might give us a better picture of how real God is.

There sat a jolly Ghost, glorious to see; who bore a glowing torch, in shape not unlike Plenty's horn, and held it up.

"Come in!" exclaimed the Giant Ghost, "Come in! And know me better, man!"

The Spirit's eyes were clear and kind. He was clothed in one simple green robe, or mantle, bordered with white fur. His feet, observable beneath the ample folds of the garment, were also bare; and on his head he wore no other covering than a holly wreath, set here and there with shining icicles. His dark brown curls were long and free; free as his genial face, his sparkling eye, his open hand, his cheery voice, his unconstrained demeanor, and his joyful air.

I know the Spirit of Christmas Present is not God. But God is not less than the Spirit of Christmas Present. God is as interesting, unconstrained, mighty, and genuinely interested in inviting you in as this Spirit. There's no pasty, filtered, churchy light coming from him, no silly little halo, no cheesy smile, no frumpy clothes, or humiliating demands. "Have you confessed all your sins? No? Okay, well, confess them all before you come in!" God is not like that. He is as welcoming, real, and abundant as this huge Ghost with bare feet. The Spirit bellows out,

"You have never seen the like of me before!"
"Never," Scrooge said.

We would probably say the same thing. Never have we
seen the spiritual world. But that doesn't mean we're left
without evidence. If you see someone's math homework
and it's neat and clean and accurate, then you know
something about that person: they are neat and clean and
concerned with right answers. It's the same way with
God's work. When we look at the natural world we're
getting a glimpse at God. We get to look at the material
world and deduce what God is like.

We know God loves beauty because of the sunsets.
We know God has a sense of humor because of ducks,
ostriches, and people like Napoleon
Dynamite. We know God loves
intimacy because of sex. We know
God thinks we're worth reproducing
because sex produces children who look
like us. We know God loves order and
variety because of the day, night, day, night cycles, and
the winter, spring, summer, fall cycles. Regular rhythms,
regular changes. God is full of interesting characteristics.

We know
God thinks
we're worth
re-producing

We look at the earth because we want to see the
Spirit behind it all. We long to see God. But often
our perspective of the real, everlasting, spiritual stuff
is muddied. I often shake my head as I walk past the
windows of Victoria's Secret because, though they can sell
sexy clothing, they cannot sell acceptance, faithful love, or
long-lasting romance.

These sorts of things are not found in malls. They are found in Jesus, who came so that we can have a full and abundant life, beyond anything we could have dreamed of.

And guess what? This real, better-than-you-ever-dreamed-of life starts today. It's what Christmas is all about. Christmas is about enjoying Jesus, the Uber-Spirit, the ultimate Being, the most real and welcoming of all people. Christmas is about remembering that thing called the Incarnation, when Jesus who was spirit took on flesh and entered planet earth in an unwed teenager's womb.

# Gift of vulnerability
*By Jonalyn Fincher*

I have a friend who trades with me. It has taken us four years to get to this point.

We have sons close in age so on Tuesdays we swap the boys. Once, when she wanted some alone time, she asked me to watch her son for 45 minutes. I was happy to help.

My husband and I loaded up the one-year-old boys and took them to the park. We watched them giggle over the heights of the swing as we pushed them up into the last rays of the sun.

> She gave us the gift of receiving our gift, and receiving well, with grace and gratitude.

We trotted them over the bridge to the library's warmth where we played Dora on the computer and put books into the children's book drop over and over.

Before I knew it, before we'd had a chance to really explore the millions of Legos strewn in the playroom, my friend came back, nails sleek and shellacked, ready to claim her little one. It was when I saw her smile that I realized she had given something to us.

She gave us the gift of receiving our gift, and receiving well, with grace and gratitude. We gave her time to be a mom who (in her words) is safe for one more day from mom jeans and a scrunchy.

Have you considered how most gifts can't be wrapped in paper and bows? Consider how difficult it really is to give things like:

time
attention
questions
thoughtfulness
words
health

You could even title this list "The Gifts of Vulnerability" for each of them require friendships with safety, peace, mercy, joy, hope — all the things Jesus meant to bring into our lives. As he put it, "Here I am! I stand at the door and knock. If anyone hears my voice and opens the door, I will come in and eat with him, and he with me" (Rev 3:20). To be with Jesus means we set our phone down, we pull our shoes off, we sit and have warm soup and bread with him.

Immanuel (God with us) means we are safe to be needy without fear, because fear is the thief that comes to kill, steal, and destroy. The evil one's work creates fear and guardedness. As my mother-in-law would say, "Is something killing you, or stealing from you? That is the work of the thief. It is not from God."

Like last week, when I needed God's comfort through the friendship of good friends, I realized that those I actually called for help, those closest to me, were women I can cry with and not fear judgment or quick-fix instruction. They image God's hope and mercy, love and peace.

They are friends who rarely misunderstand or offer unsolicited advice. They are friends who encourage my instincts, validating my thoughts and feelings.

We need to ask and receive to see how much friends can give. Think about your friendships. Who can you be honest enough to cry with? Who can you cry with and not feel like you must apologize for your tears? Who can you share a need with so that they can fill it?

This last one can be tricky because we don't want to demand our friends meet all our needs. Here are some ways you can give the gift of vulnerability to your friends this Christmas.

- I have company coming tomorrow and it would be a huge help if I didn't have (insert child or dog's name here) running around my legs. Any chance I could drop him by your place for two hours tomorrow?

- I've missed cross-country skiing (insert hobby/art/ sport) so much. I was thinking we could both go cross-country skiing. I'm free Tuesday morning. Any chance you could join me?

- My friend/husband/family member just leveled me. I think I need someone to tell me if I'm going crazy. Do you have a moment for me to tell you what happened?

- My husband and son are sick and I need to get to the store. I was wondering, if I text you a list of groceries, could you pick them up for me? I can swing by this afternoon and get them.

For me, it's an honor to know a friend is close enough and open enough with me to ask. It comes as a great compliment. It means that I make them feel like they can be honest about what they need.

And Christmas, if anything, must begin with our acceptance of gifts bigger and better than we ever thought possible.

# Winter Without Christmas

*By Dale Fincher*

The snow is aglow on Mammoth Mountain. In the Sierra Nevada mountains of Northern California, the brilliance of the moon and stars that rule the night cascade down upon rippled swells of rocks and gullies. Still as breath, these austere mountains under thick blankets of white powder stand with their peaks to the heavens in silent reverence to the One who made them.

Though the scene draws my eye and moves my soul, I am thankful that the winter is not merely about snow on mountains. If a deeper meaning were not given to this kind of beauty of rock and frozen ice, it could well be a curse to the longing of the heart. This is instantly what the children felt when they crossed from our world into Narnia in C.S. Lewis's The Lion, the Witch, and the Wardrobe. They felt the cold on their faces and in their hearts when they learned that the White Witch cast a spell on Narnia to make it "always winter and never Christmas."

That spell continues to work upon the hearts of the sons of Adam and the daughters of Eve. For some, the white mountains are the sum total of the season. Atheists and nature religions celebrate it as Winter Solstice. Religions around the world also tell their own stories of the season with Hanukkah, Christmas, Yule, and Kwanzaa. For secular societies, all these festivities and remembrances are lumped together as a simple "Happy Holidays," unaware that "holidays" comes from the word "holy days."

But not all stories were created equal. In the name of political correctness, the most important story can be squeezed out in the name of equal rights. That story of

God coming down to humans to lift all humans up is the best news we need to hear. If it is a true story, then it has the power to break the illusions of any culture, including our own, and liberate the human heart.

*If it is a true story, then it has the power to break the illusions of any culture, including our own, and liberate the human heart.*

This advent season let us not repeat the desperate question of Mary Magdalene at the empty tomb, "They have taken my Lord away, and I don't know where they have put him."1 Though it may feel this way in western society with Santa Claus and reindeer lining the aisles from early October, we can peel away the disguises placed upon Christ's coming and see it for its worth. Wherever they are, followers of Christ can remember again, despite all the trappings, that God touched down and gave us his son. As the songwriter puts it,

> I wonder as I wander out under the sky
> How Jesus the Savior did come forth to die
> For poor ordinary people like you and like I
> I wonder as I wander out under the sky.2

As we behold the winter wonderland in our part of the world, bend your gaze again toward that sky where that one bright star once shown. Remember again the Savior in swaddling clothes. Taste afresh his salvation that no commercialism, spell, or political correctness can ever diminish.

"Mary and Minute Rice"
t.oulation.org/mary

1John 20:13 NIV
2I Wonder as I Wander by John Jacob Niles

## The Traveler's Feet
*By Dale Fincher*

God touched down, sheathing himself in skin through the womb of Mary, purposing his heart toward the redemption of men and women. This was no easy task. Not only did he empty himself by limiting his attributes,[1] but he purposed himself in a single direction. Luke says Jesus increased in wisdom and stature and in favor with God and man.[2] Jesus enjoyed growing up while embodied as a human.

Can you see Mary nursing Jesus, picking him up when he cries, and changing his swaddling clothes? Then the day comes when Jesus rolls over and learns to wiggle his knees and elbows into a crawl. And, if they had cameras, surely the shutters would have been snapping the day the little Messiah took his first steps.
And those steps were his first toward the Cross. As songwriter Rich Mullins put it,

> I can see some Traveler's footprints;
> There's a little bit of blood in every step
> He made.
> I wonder what kind of burden He's bearing;
> That's cut him so deeply every step
> along the long, long way.[3]

The metaphor is a deep reminder that every place the feet of Jesus took him was part of God's conspiracy to win the world. They were steps of compassion and healing. They took him into his own country where he was received without honor. They led him into the temple where he argued vigorously over the Pharisees but had to lose himself in the crowd to avoid a premature death. They humbly accepted washing by the hair of one who had been forgiven much.

> Every place the feet of Jesus took him was part of God's conspiracy to win the world.

Then those same dust-covered feet led him to Jerusalem, to the upper room, into the garden, through arrest, and ultimately nailed to timber at the Place of the Skull.

Rich Mullins continues to give us the imagery of Christ, the Traveler:

> In the west I see an evening,
> The scarlet thread stretched beneath
> the gathering dark.
> Red as the blood on the hands of
> the Savior,
> Rich as the mercy that flowed from his
> broken heart.4

This time of year is a celebration of God's arrival to earth. Yet it is only the beginning of his journey as he grows, bleeds, empathizes, and redeems. And all for us, who humbly allow our feet to walk with him.

1 *Philippians 2:6*
2 *Luke 2:52*
3 *"The Howling" by Rich Mullins*
4 *Ibid.*

# Welcome to Tinseltown
## *By Dale Fincher*

Christmas songs once abounded in ages that now seem forgotten. They slipped out of vogue when the modern songs with the chocolaty voices began singing about other features of Christmas, like whiteness, cold, and reindeer. Today the Christmas hymns have turned instrumental in the shopping malls and boutiques. But the airwaves are full of the words of other Christmas-season songs that describe tinsel, branches, and fruity hot drinks.

> The surface-feature is the clothing a thing wears.

The essence of Christmas has been replaced with what philosophers call the "surface-features" of Christmas. The surface-feature is the clothing a thing wears. It would be like appreciating an antique car simply for its color, not for its vintage; like appreciating your wife, not because of her commitment, but because of her shoes; like celebrating a birthday by enjoying the cake, but ignoring the honored guest.

In the northern regions of the Northern Hemisphere, snow falls and folks cozy around the fireplace. Hot apple cider is the drink of choice during the opening week of winter. Sleighs were once drawn out of barns, though today cars are drawn out of garages. These coincidences, though they may be part of the winter season for many, are not Christmas.

It rarely snows in Bethlehem. Humans in many places have done a fantastic job in exalting in the trivial so as not to be offensive to those who do or do not believe in the real substance of Christmas. Let's build a snowman, comes the anthem. Hear the sleigh bells, resounds another. Let Christmas be white, exclaims yet a third. And the surface-features so clothe the proper holiday that the substance under the clothing becomes hollow.

The happiness over winter has, in some sense, replaced the joy of a visiting God, and for all the busyness at the malls and on the airwaves, the celebration has become confusing.

One Christmas I was privileged to sail on a family cruise in Central America. On Christmas Eve, when many followers of Christ around the world were going to midnight services for quiet and worship, the guest entertainment host on our ship led us through a myriad of secular Christmas-time songs. Guests belted out songs about Frosty and Santa and Rudolph. "I'll Be Home for Christmas" lulled with irony as I looked at other guests who were clearly not home for Christmas. I scanned the faces of the red-and-green-dressed audience that evening. The songs fell quietly upon desperate countenances that seemed to say, "Is this all there is?" Christmas, for them, was quickly consumed.

J. B. Phillips says, "We must never allow anything to blind us to the true significance of what happened at Bethlehem so long ago." But many of us have. Sadly, today's secular Christmas is a holiday as substantial as the stuff of tinsel.

Remember we live on a visited planet.

How do we peel off the layers of triviality that encumber us? To remember we live on a visited planet, which is founded on reasonable evidence and good testimony. This visit, though two millennia ago, is not insignificant in light of the promises that the infant-Child-turned-Savior gave us. As Christoph Blumhardt notes, "We must speak in practical terms. Either Christ's coming has meaning for us now, or else it means nothing at all." Time cannot reduce he who is Eternal.

There is nothing wrong with the surface-features of Christmas, like there is nothing wrong with a color of a car. But when we equate the surface-features with the Thing itself, we miss the point. The world's heart is already broken. The world still needs to see that the atmosphere of Christmas is inconsequential to the substance of Christmas.

Let us be deliberate about pausing to look up at the stars. Those are the ones Abraham saw. Followers of Christ are counted with that number. That sky is also where the Magi found the location of the God-Man. Let us also be deliberate to remember, not just the infancy of Christ, but the gargantuan plan of God's Kingdom—the downward mobilization to give us citizenship to a Country that needs no tinsel.

# Star of wonder
### *By Dale Fincher*

The angels were not the cute little baby ones we find on postage stamps. These were obvious, brilliant, and startling beings. They came to a field. They came at night. The glory of God shined from them. Without intention, they terrified the shepherds in the field. Their first words, "Fear not!" If they came today, SETI would be on the case.

Luke said the sheepherders lived in that field. Herod the Great lived in the local palace. However, God is not impressed by rank or role. God sees all humans alike, as image bearers with hearts, hands, and hair. He sees them for who they are, the choices they make, the character of soul they have become. He sees if they have a posture of humility or pride toward him.

> God sees all humans alike, as image bearers with hearts, hands and hair.

Herod (self-proclaimed, "the great") had no such posture. When he heard the headline from the Magi that a Messiah was born, he told wise ones he wanted to know the location of the child so that he could demonstrate a posture of humility in worship. But as the story unfolds, we find that Herod's aim was to eradicate the news with infant genocide. Songwriter Rich Mullins echoes Matthew and Jeremiah when he writes about the ancient event:

Rachel is weeping for her children that she thought she could not bear,
And she bears a sorrow that she
cannot hide....[1]

Imagine the heartache that ripped through the city as Herod stole the lives of children and the hearts of mothers. Herod was filled with contempt for a baby who bore the best spiritual, moral, political, and social good news. Herod not only wanted to rid Palestine of Jesus, but had he succeeded, he would have robbed the world of something Herod could have never given: a Savior who is Christ the Lord.

In contrast, the Magi, who were Zoroastrian priests, were not threatened by an announcement of the Messiah, the Chosen of God. They were waiting for the ruler of the world. A prediction of a rare joining of Jupiter and Saturn was recorded in Cuneiform tablets in 8 B.C. Jupiter (which meant "world ruler") and Saturn (which was the star of Palestine) met in the sky known as "the Fishes" (which indicated the last days). This only takes place every 794 years.2 That is why the wise Magi traveled from the East in search of Jesus at the capital of Palestine. They wanted the ruler to come. Matthew says they engaged in the humble act of worshipping Jesus, the newborn world ruler.

Still, the only formal announcement came to some ordinary guys watching sheep in a field, like servants in a banquet hall. These were men who spent their days in wool more than in books, like the guy who put up my fence or the guy who pulled the stumps from my backyard. It would be strange to my contemporary ears to hear my painter tell me about a birthday announcement from angels in his backyard while he flipped burgers for dinner. I'd doubt and go online to verify the news.

These Jewish shepherds witnessed the largest choreographed dance of angels ever recorded. As bewildered as they were, they still ran to see an even more interesting event. Luke says that after visiting the baby Jesus, they "returned, glorifying and praising God for all the things they had heard and seen, which were just as they had been told." Even the shepherds ran to verify the message of the angels. And they met Jesus face to face and believed.

[1]"Jacob and 2 Women" by Rich Mullins
[2]Michael Green, Who Is This Jesus?, 24, 25. This coincidences of stars is not a verification the world ruler will be born every 794 years. Rather, God's fullness of time, bringing his Son into the world, gave a hint to the Gentiles who lacked knowledge of the scripture.

## Custom-made care
*By Jonalyn Fincher*

When any two people as lovers, as friends, as family take time to know one another for the purpose of working good in each other, then love is taking root in their lives.

Love flourishes when I become a scholar of my sister; it grows when she wants to know me. The gifts I give her will show her how well I'm getting it right. If she likes used gifts above new ones, then the day I give her our used car seat for her new baby will actually be a day of victory for us both. She will look at me and know that I know her well.

Love is growing between us, even if I would have preferred to purchase a bright, clean, new one.

Most people would agree that God is, of all things, love. Many Christians will go on to say that God is all-knowing. Put the two together and it makes sense that God can give some stunningly appropriate gifts. He doesn't need marketing ads to help him purchase the item that will bring that smile to our faces or that glow of delight when we rip the package open. God doesn't need our Christmas list. He knows how to give great gifts because he knows us! Mary recognized this and praised God for giving her a son who would be the Messiah, singing: "From now on all generations will call me blessed, for the Mighty One has done great things for me."1

But the sad, strange observation I've made of Christmastime is that Jesus is not seen as a gift given in love. He's seen as a stumbling block. We sometimes hear questions like, "Why is there just one way to God? Why can't all religions lead to God?"

G.K. Chesterton responded well to this objection, "We should not complain that there are not ten ways into heaven. Instead, we should be grateful that there is at least one." If God wants our good, then it is for our good that there is only one way to heaven.

> If there is only one way to heaven we can be assured that his one way is precisely what we need.

Can we really be glad for the gift of exclusivity? Can we really say God knows us best; he is the best lover of our souls, both in this life and the next? If there is only one way to heaven we can be assured that his one way is precisely what we need.

But we don't do well with accepting God's gifts. For instance, for those born without physical disabilities, don't we know the critical gaze we give our own bodies? How often do we ridicule our physical appearance?

Based on our discontent with the look of our own bodies we laugh at ourselves. Or we joke that God got distracted when he made our nose, or our toes, or our hair. Remember Anne Shirley, "God made my hair red on purpose and I've never cared for him since."

James says that every good and perfect comes down from the Father of lights who does not get distracted or change his mind. I think it would be safe to say Jesus is about the best and most perfect of all gifts in our lives. Jesus is more perfect than our spouse, than our church, than our talents, than our families. Jesus was customized for our needs on planet earth.

Jesus draws us uniquely using the Spirit's distinct work in each of our lives. Jesus can speak through a faithful pastor, a pagan prophet, or a still small voice. He won't be contained by exclusive methods, but his exclusive claim to be able to flip the switch in our souls from off to on remains one-of-a-kind.

As we enter into knowing and loving God, he takes us on our own adventurous walk to places we wouldn't have expected.

Perhaps of all answers I've studied to explain why there is only one way to God, the best ones point back to the work Jesus has done in me. If Jesus can change me this much, why wouldn't I expect his power to work for every person on this blue planet? And how could I fault him for wanting to give the gift of himself to them too?

"My dear, dear friends, if God loved us like this, we certainly ought to love each other... if we love one another, God dwells deeply within us, and his love becomes complete in us—perfect love!

This is how we know we're living steadily and deeply in him, and he in us: He's given us life from his life, from his very own Spirit. Also, we've seen for ourselves and continue to state openly that the Father sent his Son as Savior of the world. Everyone who confesses that Jesus is God's Son participates continuously in an intimate relationship with God. We know it so well, we've embraced it heart and soul, this love that comes from God."[2]

If Jesus can change my disgust into love, if Jesus can take away the sting of death and join us into a never-ending relationship with the Godhead, if Jesus can reclaim our human identity from corruption to nobility once again, then perhaps he knows enough and can love enough to do the same for everyone—every single person on this earth who believes that God is a giver of good gifts.

[1] Luke 1:48-29 NIV
[2] 1 John 4:11-16 The Message

# No minutes to spare
*By Jonalyn Fincher*

I can identify with Mary, expecting a boy, and the inconvenience of being pregnant and having to travel. Nazareth is 80 miles from Bethlehem, a distance in the first century that she could have covered in one week at best.

Today, Mary's journey to Bethlehem would be tantamount to me learning that a new tax law required Dale and I to fly standby to Alaska for registration a week before my due date. The kicker: there's no room in any inn, so we'd have to stay, and give birth to our firstborn son, in the janitor's closet of a Motel 6.

If that was what God had in store for his son, I would certainly wonder, "Couldn't you, the Maker of all things, orchestrate the arrival of the Son of God a little more majestically?"

Mary only got one dream from the angel Gabriel, only one customized message for her ears, ordered by God to explain this Holy-Spirit-produced baby in her body.

> Mary only got one dream from the angel Gabriel ... Joseph got four ...

Joseph got four dreams, explaining where to move, when to leave, how to find safety, and what God was up to. I think I would have felt a little gypped, but Mary didn't.

How did she do it?

How did Mary have the strength to bear the Son of God and the serenity to respond to Gabriel's shocker of a newsflash with, "I am the Lord's servant, may it be to me as you have said?"[1]

Mary was not just a careless teenage woman pregnant outside of marriage. She was a good Jewish woman pregnant outside of wedlock.

As a Jew, she would have been familiar with one passage in the Jewish scriptures that must have made her last minute trip to Bethlehem a little easier to swallow.

"But you, Bethlehem Ephrathah, though you are small among the clans of Judah, out of you will come for me one who will be ruler over Israel, whose origins are from of old, from ancient times."[2]

The majesty and poetry of these lines aside, Mary could see how the pagan Roman census was actually accomplishing God's promise for Israel. Mary knew about the God of Israel, the God who was faithful to Abraham, the God who could lift the humble up out of the pit. Mary knew her God; she also knew what her God wanted out of her.

Around Christmas time, I notice people like me running around with lists of things to do. Minute Rice put together an advertisement in 2008 that summed up the way I often feel around the holidays. Surrounding a package of Minute Rice with a Santa Hat are hundreds of things to do, including things like:

*get decorations out of the attic, sew angel costume for Molly's pageant, write annual holiday letter and try to sound modest while bragging about the kids, drop off food at church, buy poinsettia plants, hang candy canes, try not to eat candy canes, clean house, keep tinsel away from cat, shop online during lunch hour, buy stocking stuffers, drive around and look at lights, plan menu for Christmas Eve, make punch for party, have patience when visiting in-laws, read "Night Before Christmas" out loud, attend candlelight service with family, remember reason for the season, pray for peace on earth.*

Minute Rice promises that they are here to help. Great.

That last item on the list makes me stop and wonder, *how on earth can you pray for peace when your life has no peacefulness in it?* There's no shalom, the kind of peace that envelops every dimension (spiritual, physical, political, economic, emotional, social) in this ceaseless running-around living.

I think that if Mary had a Minute Rice list, she must have scrapped it so she could make time for the Son of God to enter her life.

I recently found that Micah doesn't merely contain prophecies about Bethlehem, it also has a better to-do list. One that I'd like to recommend this Christmas to all those women (and men) out there who find there is just too much to do.

"He has showed you, Oh man, what is good. And what does the LORD require of you? To act justly and to love mercy and to walk humbly with your God."[3]

Three items.

What would it look like if we acted with justice, loved with mercy, walked with humility this Christmas? And scratched all the rest. Can you imagine how much more fun we'd be having?

I can.

[1]*Luke 1:38 NIV* [2]*Micah 5:2 NIV* [3]*Micah 6:8 NIV*

# Love needs knowledge
*By Jonalyn Fincher*

Think of those you might need to be more proactive to love, those family members who strike you as constantly annoying or just plain difficult to get close to. Christmas isn't simply about a sweet baby lying in a manger; it's about love made flesh, taking hands and feet and invading our everyday lives. When God's love touched down on earth we received the supernatural fuel to consistently, sacrificially, unconditionally love.

> Christmas isn't simply about a sweet baby lying in a manger; it's about love made flesh

Perhaps those couples who have braved decades of marriage together know more about this kind of fuel than anyone else. I've heard elderly couples reminisce about their early married years. "Oh, we barely knew each other back then." And they laugh at their silly expectations and demands on each other. Then sometimes you catch a glimmer of knowing in an exchanged glance or a slight squeeze as they hold hands. If there is closeness between them, it is because they know each other so much better.

With over a decade of marriage under my belt, I know my husband much more than I did on my wedding day. That knowledge works itself out in practical terms. One year I learned that he likes a certain kind of toothpaste more than the sparkly sweet flavors I used to buy. That means I have more power to love or annoy my husband.

What do we do with the knowledge we have of those in our family? How do we will their good with what we y of them? Do we insist that our desire is their good, we keep pressing to know them, studying them would a great story that's always changing? One thing I've noticed is how easy it is to fail to "update" our knowledge of family members, assuming that how they were 10 years ago is how they are now and how they will always be. It comes out in phrases like "Oh that's just Uncle Cain. He's always been a murderer, always will be." But perhaps Uncle Cain has repented this year and wants the chance to be re-known by his family. If we refuse to update our knowledge, then we have refused to know and thereby refused to love.

Loving isn't always being present; loving might mean leaving. There are times when my presence is not good, not necessarily because I'm a mess, but because I can stand in the gap where God wants to work. When I'm gone from my husband, for instance, he has the space to be in uninterrupted solitude, to write, to fish, to fix up his Jeep, to read, and to relax. He has time to be loved by Another. Mothers know this well when they let their children grow up. Fathers know this when they allow their son to confront the bully on his own.

We are not capable of being all the good in anyone's life. Because we are finite beings our companionship has its limits. When we allow God in, he will fill up the corners where our love is deficient. We can trust him to love supernaturally. And trusting Christ to love another that I desperately want to love is part of my love for them too. But often, I have to get out of the way, to be proactive about pulling away, to love by removing myself. I withdraw, even though sometimes I really don't want to, so the Infinite God can take over, loving where I am deficient, encouraging where I cannot, filling the souls of the hungry.

It would be a relief if we could get a tick-off list of what love must always include, but there is no one-size-fits-all list. The way to love this person or that annoying family member is unique to them. Love must be free to customize itself to the beloved and his unique needs, taking different pathways depending on whom we love and who God has asked us to be in their lives. There is only the guideline that love requires knowledge.

Love must be free to customize itself to the beloved

The way I love my husband now is different from how I loved him when we were just getting to know each other. We're both glad for the improvement. Love requires that we keep a listening ear to how God wants this person's good. It probably will look unexpected too, a little like Mary sitting in the straw of a dusty, dark stable wondering what had become of her neat trajectory.

And when we are weak, which we will be in just a few more hours, we can walk with confidence over to God's well, where because of Jesus we can dip our jars again and again, knowing there are everlasting cisterns of love from which we can fill buckets.

MESSIAH

## Light in Darkness
Isaiah

The people walking in darkness
have seen a great light;
on those living in the land of the shadow of death
a light has dawned.

You have enlarged the nation
and increased their joy;
they rejoice before you
as people rejoice at the harvest,
as men rejoice
when dividing the plunder.

For as in the day of Midian's defeat,
you have shattered
the yoke that burdens them,
the bar across their shoulders,
the rod of their oppressor.

Every warrior's boot used in battle
and every garment rolled in blood
will be destined for burning,
will be fuel for the fire.
For to us a child is born,
to us a son is given,
and the government will be on his shoulders.
And he will be called

Wonderful Counselor, Mighty God,
Everlasting Father, Prince of Peace.

Of the increase of his government and peace
there will be no end.
He will reign on David's throne
and over his kingdom,
establishing and upholding it
with justice and righteousness
from that time on and forever.
The zeal of the Lord Almighty
will accomplish this.

(Isaiah 9:2-7 :: TNIV)

"Love: Stripping Away the Disguises"

soulation.org/disguises

## Dale & Jonalyn Fincher

speak and write nationally as a husband-wife team through Soulation (Soulation.org), a nonprofit dedicated to helping others be appropriately human. Their previous books include *Living with Questions*, *Ruby Slippers* and *Coffee Shop Conversations*. Their work has been featured in *Christianity Today*, *UnChristian: What a New Generation Really Thinks about Christianity*, *Apologetics for a New Generation*, *The Washington Post* and *The Wall Street Journal*. They make their home in Steamboat Springs, Colorado, with their son. They love watching *Downtown Abbey*, off-roading and hiking in the nearby aspen wood.

Special thanks to Brandon Hoops, senior editor at Soulation, who compiled this book in your hands. His eye for theme and rhythm has brought good things to our lives. He has appeared at our doorstep bearing heirloom tomatoes from his grandfather's garden and has woken us up to new ideas in his editing. We are grateful for his love for growth and words on the Soulation writing team. Hoops, thanks for gathering the pieces to make *Opening the Stable Door* possible.


In your debt,
Dale & Jonalyn Fincher

Thank you for sharing advent with us through *Opening the Stable Door*. We love feedback. Please let us know how you enjoyed this book.

To find more thoughtful, out-of-the-box resources from Soulation, visit Soulation.org. New articles and titles added regularly.

To buy this book for a friend, visit amazon.com. To purchase multiple copies for your church or reading group, please contact us for pricing.

Email:  mail@soulation.org
Mail:   Soulation
        ATTN: Opening the Stable Door
        PO Box 772574
        Steamboat Springs, CO  80487

CPSIA information can be obtained at www.ICGtesting.com
Printed in the USA
BVOW081328191112

305925BV00001B/2/P